Copyright © 2025 Stan Lake

All rights reserved.
This book or any portion thereof
May not be used or reproduced in any fashion whatsoever
Without the permission of the publisher or the author
Except for the use of quotations

Publisher: Dead Reckoning Collective
Editor: Keith Walter Dow
Book Cover: Tyler James Carroll

Printed in the United States of America

ISBN-13: 978-1-963803-11-2 (paperback)
Library of Congress: 2025945355

For more information, please visit:

deadreckoningco.com

A TOAD IN A GLASS JAR

Stan Lake

"What a pleasure to be trusted with the deepest, darkest parts of someone you think so highly of. One page, I'm in the woods, creek hopping at 12, the next had me in a Humvee, vulnerable and scared for my life. The next had me thinking about how thankful I am to live life knowing individuals like Stan Lake, a creative creator, a steward of nature, and a friend. I've always enjoyed his ramblings. I'm glad he took the time to put them all together. Like I said, a pleasure."

Aaron Penn, Vocalist for Element of One, Never In Life, End of Your Rope, and more: North Carolina Hardcore scene alumni. 1996-present.

"What I most admire about this debut collection is Stan Lake's ability to depict the suffering of human existence, yet also depict the wonder. *A Toad in a Glass Jar* is especially valuable for those who struggle in the aftermath of trauma, because Lake's often gritty poems are those of a survivor. Ultimately, these poems bring darkness into the light. They inspire."

Ron Rash, Author of *The Caretaker* and *Serena*

"Structured as a four-act journey, Stan Lake's *A Toad in a Glass Jar* follows a life from wild creeks to war and its aftermath. In the first act, Beginnings, the eponymous poem addresses themes of captivity and exhibition—visibility without agency. Larval Phase recalls the feral boy who climbed cedar trees "long before the war," when fear had not yet learned his name. Metamorphosis confronts the theme of return with the line, "I'm circling the drain again," expressing a raw honesty that avoids theatrics. The final Act, Adult Phase commits to acceptance, forgiveness, and growth—"I'd rather hear your complaints / than speak / at your funeral"—choosing connection over silence.

A lifelong hunter of toads, snakes, and lizards, Stan writes with the precision and attentiveness of a field naturalist. The herpetology in his work isn't mere decoration but a lens—often clouded by southern mud and desert sand—through which he teaches us how to see. Part naturalist's notebook and part after-action report, this book prioritizes witnessing over spectacle and life over the unsent letter. For anyone who has felt both caged and called, these poems offer a path forward: kneel by the creek, lift a stone, and keep looking."

John A. Dailey, Author of *Tough Rugged Bastards: A Memoir of a Life in Marine Special Operations*

"*A Toad in a Glass Jar* bleeds authenticity from the first page to the last. Stan Lake's talent and experience intersect beautifully in this heartfelt collection that navigates tales of joy, pain, and everything in between."

Scott Blackburn, author of *It Dies with You*

"In *A Toad in a Glass Jar*, Stan Lake traces a life through four acts of transformation—childhood wonder, the crucible of war, the shadows of survival, and the long march toward making peace. His poetry is accessible yet unflinching, grounded in raw honesty and sharpened by moments of lyrical imagery. These poems weave nature, conflict, grief, and resilience into a candid portrait of what it means to grow, serve, and wrestle with memory. Both a veteran's testimony and a deeply human meditation, this collection reflects on love, loss, and the memories that refuse to stay buried—yet it never loses sight of the fragile, tenacious hope that healing is possible."

Mike Warnock, Editor-in-Chief, The Havok Journal

"Stan Lake's *A Toad in a Glass Jar* spans continents and the breadth of human experience. At once universal and deeply personal, Lake's poetry draws on his vast encounters with the natural world while offering poignant reflections on the human condition. In pieces such as "Growing Up Wild" and "War Dreams," he traces memoryscapes of childhood and conflict; in "Icarus," he contemplates the intricacies of father–son relationships. Lake moves seamlessly from moments of lighthearted delight to the depths of human struggle with an observant eye towards the earth."

Nicolette L. Cagle, author of *Saving Snakes: Snakes and the Evolution of a Field Naturalist*

"In this searing debut, Stan Lake shatters myths of war, family, and survival. *A Toad in a Glass Jar* peers through the magnifying glass of memory, revealing poems that are stark, luminous, and deeply human."

Michael Jerome Plunkett, Author of *Zone Rouge*

"Some poems in *A Toad In A Glass Jar* read like an enthusiastic science teacher motivating kids on a field trip, while others hit like a hardcore song being shouted from the pit. Stan Lake does an incredible job of shifting mood, subject matter, and meter while describing things as innocuous as seeing the vast rows of plants in a tobacco field in his youth to the ominous dead eyes of an Iraqi looking skyward. From his love of all things that waddle, slither, dangle, and creep to his childhood in NC to his experiences overseas, Stan Lake captures the full spectrum of life… and death."

Brian Sanders, Host of The Disruptors Podcast and co-host of NIGHTSHIFT with Andrea Up Late)

"Typically, we look at amphibians and insects through a magnifying glass to observe their intricacies. We zoom into the slime and amplify the seemingly disgusting, exceptional complexities. Instead of holding a magnifying glass to these creatures, Stan holds a mirror, allowing us to view our own gifts, flaws, and idiosyncrasies through the lens of these magnificent critters."

Benjamin Fortier, Award-Winning Author of *Phantoms*

"Poet and veteran Stan Lake's *A Toad In A Glass Jar* is one of the most honest and courageous collections I've read in a long time. Lake pours light into the shadowy country of the human heart, contrasting the sweetness of nature and the horrors of war, a deep longing to remember and a desperate urge to forget. These poems illuminate the paradox of beauty and violence that underlies not just a single human life, but human history as a whole. We need more poets this brave."

Taylor Brown, Author of *Rednecks* and *Wolvers*

"*A Toad in a Glass Jar* is a book of poetry to be felt as much as it is read …. It's like a companion for anyone who has ever battled the darkness, longed for connection in their life, or searched for meaning in struggle. Stan Lake is one of the most sincere people I know …. in his life and in his writing … and his words carry that honesty on every page. His poetry doesn't posture or pretend. It opens a vein straight to the heart, it offers truth, and it's just as much vulnerable as it is courageous."

Joe Musten, vocalist for Advent, drummer for Beloved, and The Almost.

"As someone who conserves nature for a living and someone who has experienced the effects of suicide in my immediate family, I found that the poems in this book brought me through a series of emotions and provided an example of how a love of nature can help us heal from pain and trauma."

Dr. Christopher Jenkins, CEO The Orianne Society

"Stan's poetry is a great example of a man coming to terms with a world where he can't help but look out in wonder. His mixture of curiosity, humility, and introspection is refreshing in an age where popular culture is telling you what to see and believe. Instead, Stan looks simultaneously inward and outward, trying to make sense of it all. We need more people like Stan Lake in this world."

Dennis Lamb, guitarist from Prayer for Cleansing, Azazel, and Bedouin Temple.

EDITOR'S NOTE

I've known Stan Lake for the better part of a decade, but only met him in person for the first time in 2022 when we hosted a launch party for *Rock Eater*, by Mason Rodrigue at a dive bar in Jacksonville, NC. It would be another year after that before Stan submitted the manuscript for *A Toad in a Glass Jar* and another two before we made its final edits. He had started and finished so many creative projects on his own by this point. While editing *A Toad in a Glass Jar* we started and stopped and started again and then often stopped for a lot longer. It can be an uncomfortable process, and I imagine I took more time than he would have preferred at many of those pauses. I know that working with an editor was a welcome change, but a pace he probably wasn't used to, and he was gracious every step of the way.

As an editor and a publisher I get the privilege of pushing other people's writing across the finish line and demanding things of them they didn't even know they were capable of. In the grand scheme of human performance, our ability to perfect the written word and express ourselves in any genre is a beautiful thing to witness in its evolution. This collection of poems is about as close to a poetic memoir recounting origin to end as I've ever seen, but it didn't begin that way. I'd be lying if I said the time it took to revise it was in my plan to flesh it out, but the span of time from submission to publication was critical in its development.

Stan, like other poets I've met and worked with, knows that he can write poetry that makes him and others feel something, but it took some convincing that that's what "good art" really is. Where he truly lacked confidence was whether or not he was "doing it right." It's taken him some time to learn this, but working through this manuscript with him was a great way to show him that "right" doesn't always look the same for everyone.

These poems will move you. Whether you grew up knee deep in creeks or spent an adolescence jumping off of stages while hardcore bands deafened the room or felt like no one understood your experience or joined the National Guard thinking you'd never leave the country, they'll make you feel things. What's more, these poems will teach you. Whether you've made assumptions about someone in lieu of expressing interest, or tried to "suck it up" when you've gone through a difficult time, or spent a lifetime trying to describe the worst day of your life to someone you share a home and the majority of your day with, they'll drop some lessons in your lap. If one thing is clear, it is our collective hope that you share these poems with people who can be moved by them and learn from them.

Keith Walter Dow
Dead Reckoning Collective

ACT I: BEGINNINGS

A Toad in a Glass Jar	18
Growing Up Wild	19
By the Time I was Seventeen	20
Oh Cedar Waxwing	21
An Ode to Toads	22
Tobacco Towns	23
Icarus	24
Summer Solstice	25
Hummingbird	26
Chickadees and Daffodils	27
Mawmaw's Garden	28
Red Cardinal	29
Giant	30
I Dreamed I Saw a Turtle	31
I Hope Heaven is a Wild Place	32
Lizards	33
The Woods were Silent	34
June Bug Wind	35
Good Dog	36
Cicada Scream	37
Frog in a Boiling Pot	38
Ants	39
Like Fleas on a Dog	40
An Ode to Broom Sedge	41
Old Sages	42

ACT II: LARVAL PHASE

Long Before the War	44
One Weekend a Month	45

13 Mike Transportillery	46
Sons and Daughters	47
One Year Younger	48
A Place Older than Time	50
Oh Babylon	51
Scania Toads	52
Yellow Bird Cadence Post Service	53
Thylacine	54
Camel Spider Outside Fallujah	55
Iraqi Bats	56
A Snake in the Garden	58
Right Seat Ride	59
Qualifying Service	60
Baptized by Fire in Baghdad	61
Dead Haji	62
War Dreams	63
One Deployment	64
Homesick and Hazy	65
The Thread that Held Us	66
War is Hell	67
Time	68
Perfect in Pictures	69
Saves the Day	70
Winter Acoustic	71
Burn it All	72
August Rolls Around	73
The Hardest Part	74
Memorial Day	75
Losing Sight	76
I Lost My Heart in a Faraway Land	77
Dust	78
A Violent Poem	79

War is	80
Old News	81
Knocking on Death's Door	82
Welcome Home	84
Confederates in the Dirt	85
All They Talk About	86
Man of Faith	87
Faithless in the Fog of War	88
Am I the Enemy Now?	89
Homesick Dreams	90

ACT III: METAMORPHOSIS

Blackout Drunk	92
Circling the Drain	93
Droning On and On	94
Meditations and Lamentations	95
Silver Tongued Siren	96
Follow Me	97
And Then I Just Left	98
Almost Every Night	99
Reflected Ghosts	100
Funeral Prayers	101
Narratives	102
Swords of My Youth	103

ACT IV: ADULT PHASE

There's No Blood on My Hands	106
That Bitch, Death	107
The Cycle Repeats	108
In the Mirror	110

Dissonance	111
Doom Scrolling	112
Shotgun Epitaph	113
I Really Don't Want to Die	114
The World is Ending	115
Love Letters to Death	116
My Brother's Keeper	117
Complaints	118
The Strong One	119
Love in 4 Lines	120
Today is not the Day	121
Great Start	122
Weird Dreams	123
I've got Two Feet in the Grave	124
Monster	125
Losing Sight	126
Gnats on the Wind	127
Sometimes	128
What Weight does a Tree Carry?	130
Bottled Up	132

INTRODUCTION

To some people reading this, I may be the only veteran they know, and this may be the first book dealing with our most recent war that can't be found in the "military non-fiction" section. We have become a nation not accustomed to conversing with our neighbors. How can we understand if we don't ask? Supporting our troops can be as simple as lending a willing ear because surviving these stories can be a heavy load. Honest conversations and genuine interest can save lives, while assumptions and tropes have likely contributed to rising mental health issues. Although some poems contain acronyms and military jargon, there is no glossary–ask someone who might know and see where the conversation takes you.

According to a 2023 statistic, only 6% of the United States population were veterans. Even fewer of those served in any kind of combat role. Yet, when you hear of veteran issues in the news, it often paints a picture of brokenness. There is no glory in suicide, only tragedy. Our overemphasis on the "22 a day" mantras quoted by a culture desperate to paint veterans as broken further exacerbates the growing problem. Despite my resistance to towing the line of this narrative, I have found myself treading in the waters of intrusive thoughts and suicidal ideation at times. Writing offers me a lifeline when that darkness creeps in. As GWOT veterans, we all know someone who checked out early. Don't do it – we need you.

Even though I can empathize, I abhor the idea of suicide. It is absolute selfishness. The pain doesn't end when your life is over. You just transfer it to others. If you are struggling, get help. Find something that works for you. Bleed on the page if it keeps you from bleeding in the dirt. Confront your darkness, then conquer it. Find a community and discover ways to serve. It is harder to focus on your negative thoughts when you are helping others.

If writing is your thing, talk to your provider about narrative therapy; it can help. Groups like The Veterans Creative Arts Program and Brothers and Sisters Like These offer free online creative writing classes for veterans. Their goal is to help you process the issues surrounding military service through storytelling alongside other servicemembers.

Many other organizations exist to offer support to Veterans with their mental health issues, such as the Swamp Apes in Florida, Patrol Base Abbate, Heroic Hearts, Hunter-Seven Foundation, The Cohen Veterans Network, The Battle Within, and even the VA. There's no excuse not to use all the resources at your disposal.

Many other organizations exist to offer support to Veterans with their mental health issues, and there are a plethora of resources, and there's always someone willing to tell you all the good they've done for them. There's no excuse not to use all the resources at your disposal. Don't let your story end because you were too afraid to fight for your own life. People are willing to help, so swallow your pride and get connected. You're worth it, and the world needs to hear your story. Don't be a toad stuck in a jar. You were born to be free.

FOREWORD

I am a hunter. I kill what I profess to love. It's one of life's contradictions with which I must reckon. But before anyone condemns me for an act seen by many as gratuitous savagery, know that I kill because I love; because I understand and honor the cost of my place in this world.

I kill because I owe those countless caged and slaughtered cows I've consumed without thought, those chickens, nuggetized and deep-fried, I've dipped in a cup of neon sauce, to work and pursue and get elbow deep in the guts of a still steaming kill. I hunt because I owe it to face the blood and shit found in the truth of how I live and how animals die for my ability to do so. There is poetry in reality.

Stan Lake is a poet, undeniably a hunter of a sort. Poets move amongst us, watching and pondering and feeling. They pattern the world in which we live, looking for their moment, before pulling the trigger to reveal in but a few lines the truth they pursue.

Though not prone to going to the woods in pursuit of food, Stan finds nourishment there all the same. Stan is a naturalist with a poet's affinity for the less loved amongst us, which is how I came to know him. Watching videos of Stan teaching me about a host of generally unsympathetic creatures: snakes, frogs, toads, turtles, the occasional insect, all with an infectious glee and yes, love, I could not help but be drawn to this oversized kid with a grin as wide as my TV screen. Stan made it impossible not to look at the objects of his adoration in a new light, consumed as he is with the beauty of the world around us and determined to share it;

to make us see that loving the least among us offers us respite from the actual manifest horrors around us.

Because that's what poets do. They make us see, make us appreciate, make us confront those things that may be unseen or unknown or pointedly ignored. They offer understanding, even of things we'd prefer to discount. Stan loves the less loved, and in that, makes us love them too. That perspective makes the whole of the man all the more compelling.

Reading *A Toad In a Glass Jar*, one understands why Stan Lake loves the creatures he does. Through a tumultuous childhood, through war, through coming home, and reckoning with it all, Stan has carried a reptile on one shoulder, all cold blood and slow blinking, hooded eyes, while a songbird warbles happily on the other. In that he is all of us, but unlike those of us moving forward burdened by our silence, Stan gives words and air to the things many of us think but fear to express. That's the beauty of this assemblage of his poetry: he looks unflinchingly at ugliness and finds beauty, then shares it with us, no matter the cost to himself.

In the end, Stan Lake is holding us up before ourselves, with a grin and a twinkle in his eye, saying, "Look at this life. It's amazing and ugly and wonderful. Here's how it's unique and here's why I love it, as surely as I sometimes hate myself." A poet, a punk, a soldier, and an evangelist walk into a bar, and Stan Lake's truth is the punchline. As he says, "Please understand that these poems offer you a view into the deepest parts of me. The parts that I've often been either too scared or too ashamed to acknowledge."

A Toad In a Glass Jar is a study in bravery and kindness and generosity, but for the poet himself, that hunter of the human experience, it is simply the truth, the poet's quarry. At the end, you will look down at the still warm form of Stan's words, feeling sadness and thanks, regret and elation in equal measure, for the poet is the hunter and now, thanks to Stan Lake and his pen, you are too.

Let us give thanks.

Russell Worth Parker
Lieutenant Colonel, USMC (ret)

Act I

BEGINNINGS

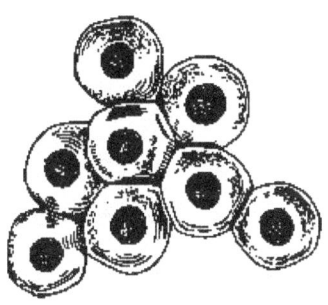

A TOAD IN A GLASS JAR

I often feel like

A toad in a glass jar.

Limitless potential

Stifled by captivity

Artificial comforts aplenty.

But a prison, ultimately

Jumping only as high

As the lid will let me.

Panoramic view

Of all the things I can't do.

I often feel like

A toad in a glass jar.

Brought around

For show and tell.

An oddity collected

But quickly neglected.

Lonely in front of many

On full display for all to see.

Stuck and listless

What an existence.

GROWING UP WILD

I grew up wild,

Feral, and free.

Long before the tendrils

Of technology.

My hours spent

Deep within wooded glens.

My brother, my sister,

My only friends.

Frogs, snakes, and box turtles we'd race

Knee deep in creeks

And other such muddy places.

I miss the days we spent

Before we had reflective faces.

BY THE TIME I WAS SEVENTEEN

By the time I was seventeen

I knew all the trees

In good ole NC

Down to species.

From bud, to bark, to leaves,

I could make a positive ID.

I don't say this pridefully

I was just good at studying

All that surrounds me, naturally.

OH CEDAR WAXWING

Previously Published in *Understory: A Digital Zine for Relief in Western North Carolina* (*Loblolly Press*)

Oh, cedar waxwing,

For what must I atone?

To live a life like yours,

Flying freely and never alone.

I find myself friendless,

Watching your aerial acuity.

In a season that feels endless,

Autumn's berries filling your pallid bellies.

Oh, cedar waxwing,

I'm flying abandoned.

My flock flew south and I'm alone.

Let me live a life like you've shown,

Surrounded by friends,

With a heart unlocked and truly known.

Seasons of solace and finding peace,

Amid the branches where you still sing.

AN ODE TO TOADS

Often, I'm asked

Why I fancy toads.

Why I'm so fond

Of hunting those wet roads.

What a weird bond I've made,

I guess you could say

I've always been fond

Of their knowing ways.

With their sidelong looks

And frowning facial display,

Quoting facts, I learned in books

And lessons learned by babbling brooks.

They just always seemed to get me,

Like we could be friends instantly.

I didn't have many friends to show

But I've always had toads.

Easy to catch and easier to like,

Toads rule my heart

On every warm summer's night.

TOBACCO TOWNS

Although I've never smoked,

I love seeing those tobacco fields.

Red Piedmont dirt supporting

That broad leaved vice,

Something about it feels like home.

Summer in the south,

A vestige of a time bygone.

The twang on my tongue

Seems to fade

The further I get

From the simplicity

Of row upon row

Of crops and old drying barns.

Home is where the heart is,

At least that's what they say.

North Carolina has my heart,

And I'm glad to call her home.

ICARUS

If Icarus

Taught us anything,

It's that seeking

The approval

Of our fathers

Can both elevate

And decimate.

SUMMER SOLSTICE

Cicadas started singing

Almost exactly

On Summer's first day.

As I sit and listen alone

I realize I've made myself

Food for the mosquitos.

It's hard to focus negatively

While nature buzzes her cacophony.

Treehoppers, crickets, and frogs

All singing their solstice songs.

Each day shorter from this day forward

Summer Solstice's song;

Just what the doctor ordered.

HUMMINGBIRD

I saw a hummingbird today.

She reminded me of you,

Perched on an empty feeder

Waiting for me to feed her.

They somehow always know

When I'm feeling the lowest of lows.

Their little hyper speed wings

Can make my sad heart sing.

I saw a hummingbird today

It reminded me I'm not through.

CHICKADEES AND DAFFODILS

Signs of spring

Like daffodils

And chickadees.

All Showing

That you're missing

All the little things.

People fail to see

Those are the things

You'll miss greatly.

MAWMAW'S GARDEN

Flowers bloom

And coffee sweet.

After the month of May

(Even if there's snow)

We had bare feet.

Tilling rows,

Catching toads.

Mawmaw's garden

Was where love grew.

Now in our hearts,

A seed's been sewn.

A memory forever,

I hope she knows.

Her impact, her value,

As my smile grows.

Flowers bloom,

And coffee sweet,

One day again,

In a garden,

We shall meet.

RED CARDINAL

I don't know what a spirit animal is

But some people say Cardinals are good to see.

That red bird's a reminder

Of people who used to be

A Southern soliloquy

Perhaps it is true

Because each time I see one

I'm reminded of you

Oh, how you loved watching

The birds and blooms

You died in spring

Which seems all the more fitting

Since now and forevermore

Each spring you're all I see

GIANT

I gave my mother away

To a giant one January day.

Now it's three decades since,

Three stepkids inherited.

"Don't call me dad, not even father,

Just to be your friend would be an honor."

He stayed true to his declaration,

Serving as a role model and inspiration.

A man of few words, his character always showed,

One of the best men I'll ever know.

Soft spoken yet a voice that could boom,

Shocked to see his round brown in their room.

This man, who wouldn't harm a fly—or me,

Was a drill sergeant in the US Army.

Crazy, how we never knew,

At six foot six, must've been quite a view.

His wild oats must have all been expressed,

Thankfully he never put me at parade rest.

I owe so much to the man he shaped me to be

All from a man who wasn't family, technically.

I was glad he didn't force a parental designation,

I consider him family, despite genetic relation.

I DREAMED I SAW A TURTLE

I dreamed I saw a turtle

In a place he shouldn't be.

He was on a sidewalk so busy,

Stuck somewhere in the periphery.

Trying to decide if the dangerous way,

Was worth a meal of blooms or some slow prey.

As he labored in the dead late winter soil,

He had the choice between smooth travel and turbulent toil.

His carapace showed signs of calloused wear,

From prior hardship, indecision, and despair.

The turtle learned long ago that scars heal,

And moving forward is the only way to his next meal.

I HOPE HEAVEN IS A WILD PLACE

When I die, I hope I find
That heaven is a real place
And that I've been found worthy.
But streets of gold and gates a' pearly
Don't really mean all that much to me.
Give me a dark rolling wood,
One with creeks and mossy logs,
Boulders and caverns and ponds to explore.
I want to spend eternity
The way I spent my childhood.
Let loose among the thorn and thistle,
Coaxing snakes and frogs from their dens.
If this were the place, I'd make eternal amends
When I shed my mortal coil
I'd love to sit by a river running rapidly.
Oh, how that'd be the way to spend eternity.
Let me have a dog or three, perhaps a pack.
We shall see.
Wild places and all who live there
Are the things I'll surely miss most.
I've heard sermons about mansions in the sky.
But, God, you can save the space!
Heaven, for me, is a wild place.
Let me dig in dirt and swim in oceans blue.
If this life is to end, I pray these things to be true.

LIZARDS

Our leaders are probably lizards,
Slimy reptilians that slither.
True intentions like chameleons,
Cold blooded, Machiavellian.

Maybe they're more like skinks,
I bet they're like skinks, what do you think?
Hiding in holes right under feet,
Awaiting an ambush for something to eat.

Perhaps they're more like monitors,
Truly undeserving of that moniker.
Forked tongues with a throaty hiss,
A mouth full of lies, so venomous.

No, they're just poor misguided men,
Preying on the weak, abiding in sin.
I wish they were more like lizards,
At least then we could kill the critters.

THE WOODS WERE SILENT

The woods were silent, not even a breeze.
No hint of wind to sway the trees.
Not a ribbiting frog to be heard.
No songs sung by soulful songbirds.
All was quiet, all was calm.
A little too quiet, I wonder what's wrong?

Children near and children far,
Pass right by, but in their cars.
Heads buried deep in digital sleep,
Not looking up, not even to peek.
Mountains and rivers passing from view,
Pass by adventures they never knew.

If a tree falls and you never saw
Will you know anything at all?
If birds all sing their last,
Will you mourn the seasons passed?
When frogs hop no more,
Will you still find them a bore?

There's a wildness yet to be tamed,
So don't get too wrapped up in your game.
Set down your digital drains,
Find your freedom out under the rains.
Get muddy, get lost, get found,
Because a child in the woods is a beautiful sound.

JUNE BUG WIND

I felt the wind
From a June bug buzzing
By my head in July.
Never seen even one
In the month of June
I wonder why.

GOOD DOG

I had a good dog,

Actually quite a few.

I've never understood,

How someone can hate dogs.

But, if my dog hates you,

Well, then I might too.

CICADA SCREAM

Cicadas are screaming.

They're in the trees.

Screaming,

From a long slumber.

Like Rip Van Winkle.

Emerging,

In the summer heat.

Cicadas are screaming.

Music to my ears.

Cacophony,

Calling for mates.

After many years celibate.

Southern songsters,

Here one day, then gone.

Aren't we all!

FROG IN A BOILING POT

A frog in a boiling pot won't jump to safety,

He will linger as the water warms hastily.

Because the pain only increases incrementally,

He doesn't register the dangers gradually.

If he were to jump into water hot,

He'd swear aloud and curse his lot.

Jumping with all his might,

Like a sticky wet bird, in flight.

The same can be said of the toad in a glass jar,

With the lid screwed tight seeing near and far.

Comfort and provision given easily,

As he dies slowly from complacency.

So, which is the greater threat,

To boil by choices made with regret,

Or be imprisoned by life's dangerous bliss,

Never knowing it won't survive death's sweet kiss?

ANTS

Sitting on my porch trying to relax,

Watching hummingbirds dive for snacks.

I stared at all the ants eating nectar on their feeder,

How can ants labor so with no leader?

There is no end to their drudgery,

As one ant becomes two, three, an army.

The banister is overrun in equal measure,

A roadway to their syrupy treasure.

I empathize, and feel like an ant sometimes,

With seemingly only two options by design.

Work 'til death, or be crushed by life.

Is there a way to savor the sweet without the strife,

Or is the pointless rhythm our only guarantee?

Perhaps tomorrow's porch observations will tell me.

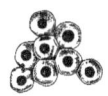

LIKE FLEAS ON A DOG

Virus or plague.
Geneva or Hague.
The Earth shakes humanity
A pestilence, like fleas, calamity.
Our penchant for pollution,
An undying love for absolution.
Battle hymns sung fervently,
As we lay waste endlessly.

No territory to dispute,
No clean water to pollute.
Corporations pumping dioxins,
Companies mining toxins.
Earth dies unhurried.
As pests multiply and scurry
She's shaking us free from her midst,
Removing our parasitic obnoxiousness.
Consumption and apathy,
Grow faster than blackened trees.
Like fleas on a mongrel dog,
She's the boiling pot, we're the frog.

AN ODE TO BROOM SEDGE

Oh broom sedge, how I love your weedy beauty.
To most, you're a blight, an unlovely sight,
But to my siblings and I, you were a fortress.
Overgrown fields full of splendor to hide us.
Moving through your shoots, hiding, and seeking.
We'd low crawl through your blonde stems,
Lobbing pinecone grenades at enemies unknown.
You sway with the autumn breeze,
Eliciting memories like an old floral friend.
I miss the days of imagination
With fields unmowed and lavishly lush.
Your seedheads with their golden tone,
Reminds me of those kids who later grew up.
Motherhood for one and warfare for two.
The three of us against the world,
Hiding in broom sedge using sticks as swords.
I miss playing war before there was a price.
There's just something about that tall brown grass,
A mystery and memories behind every blade.
Combat played as a game, with children concealed,
A preparation for the world to come.
My childhood wouldn't be the same,
Without your unkempt elegance.
Your shoots and stems were taller than we were back then,
I'd give just about anything to go back.

OLD SAGES

Robert Frost taught me
Of the world's beauty,
Swinging from birch trees,
That's what he taught me.

Wilfred Owen taught me
Of the world's cruelty,
Pro patria mori,
That's what he taught me.

William Golding taught me
Of the world's humanity,
Sucks to your asthma piggy,
That's what he taught me.

George Orwell taught me
Of the world's equality,
But some are more equal than me,
That's what he taught me.

E.O. Wilson taught me
Of the world's ecology,
Ants and their communities,
That's what he taught me.

Steve Irwin taught me,
Of the world's ferocity,
But to always love the unlovely,
That's what he taught me.

CS Lewis taught me
Of the world's divinity,
From Narnia to Mere Christianity,
That's what he taught me.

Rachel Carson taught me
Of the world's fragility,
When song birds fall silently,
That's what she taught me.

ACT II
LARVAL PHASE

LONG BEFORE THE WAR

Previously published in *Lethal Minds Journal*

Long before the war

We'd climb cedar trees so high,

We'd lose sight of the ground.

Swaying with the rhythm

Of sturdy timeless boughs,

There was no fear

In our backyard forts

With cap gun conquests

And mysteries abounding.

War was just a distant concept;

Something other people did,

Something the grown-ups did,

In some place far far away.

I miss the boy that climbed cedar trees

Long before the war.

ONE WEEKEND A MONTH

The week before

Those towers fell

I rode back from MEPS

With a recruiter.

The spawn of hell,

"What a time to sign up,"

I said in my ignorance.

Two weeks a summer

And one weekend a month.

Free college and a bonus.

I should have bit my tongue,

A week later we were at war,

This education wasn't so free anymore.

The recruiter smiled

With silvery tongue forked,

Another dumb private

Soon will report.

13 MIKE TRANSPORTILLERY

King of battle,
Follow me.
I chose the artillery,
Recruiter lied to me,
When I asked for infantry.
Said "we don't have slots
But I bet you like
To blow shit up,"
And I agreed,
I do
A lot.
Multiple Launch Rocket System:
MLRS (if you're nasty)
And just like that,
I was a, Nasty Girl, No Go,
One weekend a month,
Steel rain rocket bro.
Boom Boom Artillery
Top gun crew
Shooting rockets
In front of the brass and families
At Sicily DZ
King of battle
Follow me.
When we deployed
We forgot it all.
Traded rockets
For long hauls.

SONS AND DAUGHTERS

Sons and daughters of divorce
Raised by a global war.
Terrorism was the plot line.
Fatherless, following Uncle Sam's design.
Did we do a good thing?
Was it democracy or terror that we'd bring?
Do those patriot missiles still sing?
We tapped our own phones,
From freedom fries to predator drones
And tripped over ancient bones.
Spilling blood for empire
Breathing in those toxic pyres
Wanting VA ratings while being called a liar
Did we bring freedom's song?
Or were we conquerors in the wrong
What have we done with a war so long?
I guess time and history will tell
About our arrogance and how we fell,
About the patriotism we tried to sell,
Divided and unconquered by outsiders
Dismantled within but we're still survivors.
We just sometimes need a reminder
Cause we grew up with those latch keys,
Taking care of ourselves with solo expertise.
Because we were Sons and daughters of divorce
Raised by a global war.

ONE YEAR YOUNGER

One year younger

Always a fight.

Competition, just for spite

I enlisted the week before,

And you the week after

Those towers fell.

I just turned 18,

And you went in early.

Our dad almost served,

But our uncle sure did.

I'd max out PT,

You'd do 5 more than me.

We both joined the guard

Right before declarations of war.

We both knew we'd deploy,

Just a matter of when.

I've got your back,

And you've got mine.

Quoting Rambo: First Blood,

Again, and again

Cause "Nothing is over."

"You can't just turn it off."

Same unit.

Same deployment.

Same childhood wars.

Irish twins,

Or so they say.

You're my brother

By blood shared, and traumas seen.

I'd wave from MSR Tampa.

You're going North,

My gun truck broke down going South.

Smile for cameras in Scania.

High fives at LSA Anaconda.

I saw on the Movement Tracking System

Your convoy got a complex attack.

Burned a truck to the ground.

Frantically trying to find out,

Was my brother a casualty?

He escaped without a scratch,

But he got a CAB,

And I didn't get shit!

Always a competition,

And we both came home.

A PLACE OLDER THAN TIME

There is a place.

A place older than time.

It calls to me,

From time to time.

There is a place.

A place where history began.

It sings to me,

Time and again.

There is a place.

A place of bloodshed.

It longs for peace,

But it's only in my head.

OH BABYLON

Oh Babylon,

How you call me.

You whisper affection,

On the warm summer wind.

Each clear night when stars alight,

I see your face,

And miss your sandy breath.

I long for your jackals, foxes, and hedgehogs.

The gerbils, jirds, nightjars, and bee-eater birds.

I miss the geckos, skinks, scorpions, and toads.

I even sometimes miss those bumpy roads.

Oh Babylon,

You've got secrets to keep,

And I pray I make it back some day.

Under circumstances

Much more kind.

I'd give anything to go back,

Just one more time.

SCANIA TOADS

Have you ever heard a sound,
That turned your heart around?
Having just completed a convoy,
I heard a noise that filled me with joy.
It was a familiar trill.
Could what I'm hearing be real?
Tossing my gear in the transient tents,
I grabbed my flashlight and off I went.
My M249 slung lazily across my back.
I followed my ears after stowing my pack.
Toads were calling in Scania,
Somewhere between Basra and Nasiriya.
Spring in Iraq made me forget convoy attacks,
With yellow flowers in roadside cracks.
The MSR was like the Wild West,
But hearing the toad's calling swelled my chest.
The ancient Mesopotamia marshlands
Produced a green toad in my hands.
The deployment and exhaustion melted away.
In this moment, I was me again, in every way.
A boy in a mud puddle holding a toad.
7,000 miles from home down a dangerous road.
My heart raced, and my soul sang
As .50 Cal rounds thudded and banged.
I hit my tent and found my cot,
Barely able to sleep, but happy with my lot.
I found Iraq's only species of toad,
And tomorrow night it's back to the road.

YELLOW BIRD CADENCE POST SERVICE

A yellow bird
With a yellow bill
Sat up upon
My window sill.
I lured him in
With seeds in my feeder,
Just to watch him sing.
No longer interested
In killing anything.
Why was my youth
All about death and dying?
A yellow bird
With a yellow bill
Filled his gullet with seeds.
He flew away
After he ate his fill.
No more dead birds
On my window sill.

THYLACINE

I think a lot about the thylacine.

Forever pacing,

In footage from antiquity.

Showcasing its ferocity

In that iconic black-and-white imagery.

A moment in history

Showing a slow decline,

Of a once numerous predator.

Reduced to the by and by,

Gone in body but captured in time.

I think a lot about the thylacine

Maybe I'll share the same legacy.

CAMEL SPIDER OUTSIDE FALLUJAH

Our convoy broke down

Right outside of Fallujah.

I had my SAW slung,

At the low ready,

With a 50-round drum.

Pulling security next to my vehicle.

Out of the corner of my eye,

I saw her scurry by.

For a moment I lost my composure,

As I crept closer.

Keeping one eye on my sector,

And the other on this desert specter.

I grabbed and swatted at the camel spider,

And corralled it into a Gatorade bottle.

I threw it in my cargo pocket,

And went back to pulling security.

The shock of captivity made her shed her mortal coil.

So, I kept that huge spider as a trophy for my toil.

A few days in the heat I told SGT Charles to take a whiff.

For whatever reason he took a long sniff,

And began dry heaving on the catwalk of our truck.

All because of a dead solifugid,

A camel spider I caught outside Fallujah.

IRAQI BATS

We visited the birthplace of Abraham.

We climbed to the top of a Ziggurat.

Birthplace of civilization,

A nexus of Western religion,

And all I cared about

Was the Iraqi bat.

I found it in an acrid-smelling tomb.

There was cuneiform scrawled on the walls,

But there was also a bat hanging by her claws,

And truthfully that meant more to me

Than any dusty history.

I was stoked I got to see

An animal that wasn't so foreign to me.

I left a research lab to go to war.

I studied bats as an undergrad,

And now again, once more.

We were traveling in darkness,

Guided by the signals from SINCGARS and MTS.

We got to where those prisoners were mistreated.

At Abu Gharib, we pulled security.

As fate would have it, luck struck again.

There was another bat, that old furry friend.

Miles and miles from the last,

These little mammals made me feel normal

In the most abnormal of ways.

Smile for the picture.

Scrawl some observations,

In my dusty Rite in the Rain Journal.

Show the lab I'm still studying.

I won't let a war stop me.

There are bats in Iraq to see.

A SNAKE IN THE GARDEN

There's a snake in the garden.
I imagine he prays for my pardon.
With venom in his fangs,
He's just following those hunger pangs.
There's no malice in a bite,
Defenseless, It's just his slithery plight.
There's a snake on the trail.
Like an organic landmine laden with scales.
Just as deserving to live as you or I.
I'll keep a wide berth, and let him slide by.
I worry about this little snake.
    I pray he doesn't see shovel or rake!
There's a snake in the garden.
    I hope he appreciates our dangerous bargain.

RIGHT SEAT RIDE

Those Iowa guys
Took us for a right-seat ride.
My first mission
Outside the wire
They saved up rounds,
An extra S.A.W. drum,
And a bonus grenade.
Rear convoy security,
We lit the desert on fire.
A nocturnal serenade.
Gun truck lurching to a halt,
As the convoy rolled on.
Our first mission was their last.
So, pull pin throw grenade.
Make that saw bark one last time.
Tracers ricocheted,
The grenade shook the earth,
The radio lit up with calls.
"Did y'all hear the IED?"
We hopped in the Humvee,
Caught up to the convoy.
"Yea...we heard it..."
Our heads on a swivel,
Damn those Iowa guys.
This is going to be a wild ride.

QUALIFYING SERVICE

When asked about my service,
I have to qualify it.
Usually, I just say I was in the Army,
But omit the part
About the National Guard.
It's not that I'm not proud of my service,
But I find some think I didn't earn it.
Prior to GWOT, the guard was a joke,
And maybe some units still are.
All I know is my unit served,
Shoulder to shoulder with distinction.
Working harder to prove we mean it.
People scoff that I wasn't Airborne,
I never went to Ranger school,
Or even Air Assault.
I was a dirty no-good leg,
But those guys with fancy tabs,
And cool guy badges,
Never left CONUS.
I may not have had the best training,
But I deployed overseas when called.
I don't have elite status,
But I've got a combat patch.
I didn't kick in doors,
But I wasn't a FOBBIT.
We rode the roads all night,
Carrying shit no one needed.
The Iraqis didn't care,
About the training I received.

BAPTIZED BY FIRE IN BAGHDAD

Previously published in *Lethal Minds Journal*

Lit up by red projectile fireflies,
Dancing across dusty desert skies.
I bowed into my turret, praying for relief.
In Baghdad, I was baptized by fire.

I lost my faith somewhere outside the wire.
Mortars shrieked their deathly doldrums.
IEDs ruptured with shattering blooms.
At Al Asad, I faced my fear unflinchingly.

I lost my sense of looming dread,
Reminding myself to breathe in and out,
To survive one more day, every day.
At Camp Scania, I found hope in a toad's trill.

I lost my fear of death on a bomb-blasted highway.
When the mission ended, I lost my purpose.
At Camp Buehring, I felt the weight of finality.
We went wheels up in Kuwait; it's over, finally.

I got home and learned the meaning
Of hurry up and wait, and pray, and spiral.
My brothers have all gone their separate ways,
But I was baptized by fire in Baghdad.

Singed by flame, alone, and forever changed.
I wouldn't have it any other way.
I was baptized by fire in Baghdad,
And I, with no tribe, have tried to put the war away.

DEAD HAJI

Previously Published in *In Love…& War: The Anthology of Poet Warriors Volume I*

Like a dog, you died.
You were killed and thrown aside.
Mouth agape and rigor-mortis set.
You lay stiff-legged straight,
On the side of the highway.
Eyes wide, arms straight.
Laying, watching, you wait.
Were you screaming?
You look like you're screaming.
Eyes wide, arms straight.
Rigor-mortis mouth agape.
Why did they kill you?
Why were you thrown aside?
On the highway we found you.
Like a dog, you died.

WAR DREAMS

I started having dreams about the war again.
Out of control, can't change the pace of the trauma around me.
Can't get their faces out of my soul.
Eyes congealed black, staring up to a heaven they'd probably never taste.
Or am I the infidel destined for Hell?
I just want rest.
Close my damn eyes.
Just give me rest.
Just this one time.
Sick of the sights and sounds,
From my gung-ho youth.
Can I just have peace?
Why is that so hard?
Just a night's sleep,
Without the reminders,
Without the remnants,
Of a war I never cared about.
A cause I didn't buy into.
A duty I was skeptical over.
A mission that was unclear.
Can I just sleep?
It was only a year,
And it's shaped my entire life.
Just stop the slideshow.
Let me find peace.

ONE DEPLOYMENT

One deployment

Ain't all I ever did,

But if you want a story

It's as good as any.

People don't care,

To hear the details.

They just want to know,

Did you get any kills?

One deployment

Ain't all I ever did.

But that one deployment,

Was enough Army for me.

And I've done other stuff,

But nothing as exciting,

As that one deployment,

The only one I ever did.

HOMESICK AND HAZY

Long drives and hazy skies

Makes me miss

The war,

And the guys.

I can't swallow,

This homesick lump.

Thinking back,

On that fearful fun.

When routes went

From red to black,

And back from black to red.

We'd still get hit on the MSR

On the way there,

Or the way back.

I miss those long drives and hazy skies.

THE THREAD THAT HELD US

The thread that held us was

A thin line stitched in time.

Connecting us to a continent

We visited but never wanted.

For years we stayed close,

But families and distance both grew,

And neither of us were the friends

We once knew.

So, time stretched us like threads on a loom.

Weaving a tapestry of distance,

Reminding us only

Of the thread that once held us.

WAR IS HELL

War is hell.

But...

It can also be

A hell of a good time.

TIME

If we were being honest,

We weren't patriots.

We did nothing of note.

We were just scared of dying,

And then we weren't.

And then year-on-year,

Time piled high.

We just stopped caring,

And the clock kept ticking,

Despite heeding the call.

PERFECT IN PICTURES

It was all perfect in pictures.

But now we're just pining for purpose,

Because nothing has really made sense,

Since that season in the sand.

When all we wanted was to go home,

Now we're here living on stale history.

Neglecting the absurdity of false memory.

It all seemed so perfect in pictures.

None of us were ever heroes,

And now nothing matters.

All we were was young,

Perfect in pictures.

SAVES THE DAY

Saves the Day,

House of blues,

Mid-tour leave.

The world was,

So weird to me.

Spent my time,

Singing emo songs.

Trying to be normal,

But eying the exits,

Visualizing invisible threats.

Trash on the pavement,

The crowd closing in.

I knew I'd never,

Be the same again.

Six more months,

Back in the sand.

How much more,

Will I change?

WINTER ACOUSTIC

First chords,

"Winter" Acoustic, Bayside

Transferred,

in memory of.

Post-deployment,

Indiana

demobilization,

Camp Atterbury.

"Any words?"

"Memories?"

My camera, their memory

Well loved.

Captain Thomas.

Our casualty,

Our Chaplain.

Selfless.

No greater love,

Hammer Down.

BURN IT ALL

I came home angry.

Turned in my TA-50.

Burned my war journals.

Threw away my Class-A's.

Kept the stupid shoes,

Those stupid shiny shoes.

Gave away my medals,

Not that I earned many anyway.

Some kid thought they were cool,

I no longer did.

Shoved my combat uniforms,

And my worn-out boots,

Into a musty green duffle bag.

Sometimes I wish,

I still had those journals.

But I'm still angry,

So it goes.

AUGUST ROLLS AROUND

You always get this way,

In August, near your birthday.

I guess it's a trigger,

Or something bigger.

Some foregone, forlorn, distant past.

From a time when you felt tall,

Amid the bomb blasts.

Now you're just old,

Washed up with stories untold.

Thinking about the way back when,

Knowing you'd give anything,

To go back again.

THE HARDEST PART
Previously Published in *So Long: The Anthology of Poet Warriors VOL III*

The hardest part
Of a forever war
Is when it's all over
And you look around
And see your brothers
Broken more from life,
And the burdens they carry
Than any hardship
From that deployment.
Seeing them spiral
From disappointment and death,
From the stress of combat,
And the cruelty of life.
They were once the light
That couldn't be extinguished,
And now just a flicker.
Reduced to a diagnosis.
I pray those demons
That have hijacked their brains
Go back to hell,
And return the soldiers
Who would charge through the fire,
Just to feel the burn.
The hardest part
Came not from war,
But our return.

MEMORIAL DAY

To think
Of all the friends
Who came home,
And still died in that war.
Shells of their former selves,
Existing only in memory.
Robbed of youth and sanity.
To think,
Of all the casualties,
From a war,
That never ended
for them.

LOSING SIGHT

We followed you with blind rage.
With a taste for blood, we engaged.
All these years later, broken, defeated,
You just turned tail and retreated.

It's easy to lose sight of sacrifice,
When counting expenses and not the price.
The cost and collateral damage,
Were more than just decimals to manage.

I LOST MY HEART IN A FARAWAY LAND

I lost my heart in a faraway land.

Tucked away under bloodstained desert sand.

Now I'm back home debating whether to kneel or stand,

For flags flying low at half-mast.

Wondering if I've made an idol of this iconoclast.

A nation under a God of our own making.

With Religious zealots smiling, faking.

The land of the free

and home of the brave.

For empire,

For oil,

For desperate wage slaves,

Trying to afford the

America of dreams.

But that America is

dead, so it seems,

At least to me.

Because I lost my heart in a faraway land,

For the flag, I think I'll still stand.

Because I choose to believe,

In my sisters and brothers.

All men are created equal,

Just some more equal than others.

DUST

Long after the dust settles,

On war-torn fields of battle.

We'll still be left to hum and rattle.

With the shards of broken glass of broken men.

Left wondering if what we did back then,

Was even worth the cost and sin.

A VIOLENT POEM

Violence.

Of Action

Of thought

Of deed

Of conviction

Of constitution

Of politics

Of education.

Violence.

It's all some people will ever know.

Put the sword down,

And the violence with it.

It's time to grow old…

Violently.

WAR IS

War is death.

War is a robbed childhood.

War is a rite of passage.

War is generational.

War is never-ending.

War is all we know.

War is why we're pretending.

War is Hell.

War is paradise.

War is warmth on lonely nights.

War is hate.

War is love.

War is brothers, below and above.

War is dirty.

War is clean.

War is right.

War is left.

War is simple, except when it's not.

War is over.

War is beginning.

War is repeating.

War is endless.

War is dissonant.

War is my friend.

OLD NEWS

Old wars are old news,
When you're old and used.
Looking back nostalgically
Not because you're some flag-waver.
You just miss your youth,
And the war was a big part,
Of when you felt the most alive.
When you were "ten feet tall,
And bulletproof."
Now your knees creak,
And bring tears
To your aging eyes.
It's not the physical pain per se,
It's what it all means.
Growing old,
Breaking down,
Ineffective in every way.
A tool rusted,
A field left fallow.
You're just old news,
Like those old wars.

KNOCKING ON DEATH'S DOOR

We are knocking on death's door,

Awaiting access to the bowels of Hell.

We create a dissonant end,

To the harmony we destroyed.

Earth has been laid waste,

 In the pursuit of profit.

War and rumors of wars

Are all we ever know.

We are creatures of habit.

Creatures who destroy their habitat.

We are creatures of habit,

Creatures of war.

We terrorize,

We exploit, forevermore.

We simply lay waste.

Our hearts are desperately wicked.

We consume and kill.

We kill to consume.

We are rotting on the vine.

No, everything's not fine.

We just sit idly by.

Apathetic to the ending.

Perplexed by our rendering.

The seas are toxic.

The soil has grown infertile.

We've been crying out,

And our voices go unheard.

Nations rise up.

We quell the violence,

With more violence.

We repeat the cycle.

We repeat the cycle.

Death, destruction,

Greed, apathy.

We repeat the cycle.

We've ruined everything.

WELCOME HOME

Talked to a Vietnam vet.

I said "Welcome home,"

"In case no one told you yet."

"It's a shame how y'all were treated,"

And that I was glad to meet him.

He chuckled and smiled.

Said he'd been home quite a while,

But didn't come straight.

Decided to stay in Asia, and test his fate.

Fell in love with a local,

Had a handful of kids,

And became hopeful,

About the time the Gulf War hit.

Said by then, the sentiments shifted,

And his spirits were lifted.

All because a new war shed new light,

On the sacrifices they made, despite

Justifications of wrong and right.

CONFEDERATES IN THE DIRT

What is your heritage worth?

You sprang from the same sandy soil

As those Confederates in the dirt.

What separates you,

From grave upon weathered grave,

Under pecan trees uniformly laid?

Spanish moss whispering their iniquity,

As history often bears repeating.

You, too, fought a lost cause,

Swollen with nationalism and revenge.

God, Country, and kin to avenge.

I guess heritage repeats and depletes,

The memories of original intentions.

Will history remember you the way it does

Those confederates in the dirt?

ALL THEY TALK ABOUT

All they talk about is the war.
Time spent on foreign shores.
Their ailing bodies are blamed for it.
Failed marriages and lost jobs,
Likely caused by it.
All they talk about is the war.
Maybe that's why their best days
Are always yesterdays.
Because they used to be lions,
Or that's what they say.
All they talk about is the war,
But they never really left.
Memories of dying and death
Leaving them lonely and bereft.
Back then, always back then,
Everything and nothing made sense.
They say they'd do it all again.
All they talk about is the war,
But man, I'm so tired of those stories.
There's got to be more for me.
So, I stopped talking about the war.

MAN OF FAITH

Before every mission,
The men would pray.
My eyes stayed open,
Scoffing, I'd walk away.
I had no time for divinity,
Still, I carried a cross
In my wallet with me.
Just in case there was
Truth in the Trinity.
A good luck charm, a talisman
Just in case I got bloody.
I wasn't a man of devotion.
Mission after mission
My feeble faith eroded.
A chaplain
Who was divinely devoted
Treated me as if I were worthy.
I rode with an NCO concerned for my soul.
He tried to convert me in that dust bowl.
We discussed metaphysics and evolution,
But I wasn't ready for spiritual absolution.
Before every mission,
He'd stop and pray,
Along with the Iraqis,
Some five times a day.
Perhaps God heard him,
Because we both walked away.
I had no time for God but admired his conviction.
I carried fear in my heart, while I pondered crucifixion.
What if these men were here for more than this war?
I never thought I was a man of faith, but I don't know anymore.
Through the trial and test it made me contemplate,
Perhaps there's something to this, maybe fate.
Next time I won't just walk away.
Maybe I should pray.

FAITHLESS IN THE FOG OF WAR

Previously Published in *In Love...& War the Anthology of Poet Warriors VOL I*

I'm a heretic and a hypocrite.
Carrying the weight of the world,
And memories I can't seem to forget.
I overanalyze the trauma forevermore.
When will the horrors of war not plague me anymore?
I close my eyes,
I see the man I used to be.
The blood on the pavement,
The pressure not to just lament.
The burden of a heavy heart,
The hopelessness of being worlds apart.
I shake my fist at the sky,
Come down and save me.
Show me the love they preach about.
Come down to this combat zone,
Where there's no love to be shown.
Show me who you are.
Reach down and save me.
Bring me out of the depths.
Oh death, where is your victory?
Where is your sting?
You have been defeated.
I'm still breathing.

AM I THE ENEMY NOW?

Previously Published in *In Love…& War: The Anthology of Poet Warriors VOL I*

I never pulled my trigger.
I choked on the hair-drier-heated Iraqi dust.
I smelled the shit and diesel burning in the acrid air,
From the discomfort of my Humvee,
But I never fired a round.
Not even once.
Was I the enemy or were the people of Iraq?
How do I tell?
Are those people in the car approaching our convoy
confused citizens of this desert hell?
Or are they intent on hurting me?
Should I shoot?
Can I engage?
How will I know?
Maybe I'll throw a rock and if they keep coming then I'll shoot.
Their windshield shattered.
Ok, they stopped.
Whew, that was close.
Am I the enemy now?

HOMESICK DREAMS
Previously Published in *War…& After: The Anthology of Poet Warriors VOL II*

I dreamt about you again,
With your age-old violent sand
Blowing above desert scrublands,
And groves of lush green date palm stands.
I felt homesick for your dysfunction and death again.
I grew sick in my dream longing to see them,
My brothers, now scattered on those arid Arabic winds.
Time, distance, and change are all you are to me now.
Like a warm, blood-soaked, blanket on a cold night,
You comfort me with your ancient trauma.
I miss those frightful nights and boredom days.
I long for the camaraderie and sibling rivalry.
The shared disdain for our big Army family.
I always wake up missing you,
And feeling like I still owe you.
As if I haven't done enough for your cause.
Because my brothers kept the fighting going on,
Years after I left to go back home.
To my other life, The "normal" one,
Or so I thought years and miles removed.
Who knew the real war wasn't in that distant dirt?
But in the memories, in the restlessness, in the hurt.
Wipe the sleep from my eyes,
And feel the creak in my knees.
I'm home now, no longer overseas.
The truth is that I've been homeless since I left you.

ACT III

METAMORPHOSIS

BLACKOUT DRUNK

I came home at the end of August.
I turned 23.
I recall feeling lost.
Everything I knew seemed to be gone.
I kept everyone at arm's length,
Erecting walls.
Sleeping days away.
After a brief celebratory homecoming
I didn't know what to do with,
I fell into a deep despair.
I stayed drunk for the year.

Having tasted dangerous freedom,
Standing behind ma deuce,
As we secured our convoys.
Then everything back home was gray,
And I couldn't believe anyone understood.
I was somebody,
Or at least I was to someone.
Now I'm home,
With nothing,
And no idea who I am.

CIRCLING THE DRAIN

I'm circling the drain again.

But nobody notices,

'Cause I've got this Cheshire grin.

I've let the war creep in, again.

Like those tiny grains of sand and sin.

Into my soul, they'll crawl right in.

Boring that eternal empty hole.

I shake my fists at God, at war, at you.

I fill the void with apathy, anger, and tattoos.

It seems I'm not the only one to always lose.

I need a win, a friend, a reason to begin…Again.

But each day, like the last, is gray and bleak.

Seconds to minutes, hours to weeks.

I live life on a skipping record's repeat.

Purposeless wandering,

Mission-less wondering.

Restless and resentful, chasing that adrenaline.

Wishing I could be young again.

To choose it all over, again and again.

Not changing a damn thing.

Just to feel alive one more time.

I'm circling the drain again,

But nobody notices.

DRONING ON AND ON

Blind loyalty

To your party lines

Only maintains

The status quo.

There is no value

To human life.

We've been taught

To dehumanize,

And defeat.

But we are our worst enemies.

When we don't demand change,

There is blood on your hands.

There is blood on your hands,

There is blood on your hands.

Do you hear the children cry?

As your drones strike.

That old by-and-by.

MEDITATIONS AND LAMENTATIONS

Meditate

Asphyxiate

Contemplate

Disassociate

Depression turns to Dissonance

Meditate

Asphyxiate

Contemplate

Disassociate

Equilibrium turns to imbalance

Meditate

Asphyxiate

Contemplate

Disassociate

Repetition turns to isolation

Try again.

SILVER TONGUED SIREN

Silver-tongued persuasion

From that old serpent savior,

Bidding me to dance with his mistress.

Her elegant beauty beckons and calls.

She waltzes across war-torn craters

Of my inner being.

Those thoughts I push down.

Pack my memories down;

Repress,

Repeat,

Resume.

A song that blows on the breeze,

From the pitch-perfect lungs of death.

She makes it all seem so easy.

Her master slithers and writhes,

Setting the course and tempo of her song.

FOLLOW ME

I've murdered the man I used to be;

Mercy kill

Ever so quickly.

Let the dead bury the dead,

As I've heard it said.

I confessed my iniquity,

Knowing I'm unworthy.

But I heard a still, small voice.

I barely had a choice.

He said follow me.

So, for now,

I'll conceal my apathy.

AND THEN I JUST LEFT

I can't say when it happened.
Brick by brittle brick,
The foundation crumbled.
I preached to thousands.
Bills left unpaid; wife resentful,
I was humbled,
And then I just left.

Family over "calling."
Lifted pound by pound.
I once was lost…now I'm found.
Started living my own truth,
Not the dogma from the pews.
The church stopped calling,
And then I just left.

Sat for sermons on giving,
And some on serving the poor.
When God closes a window…
He also closes that door.
I've gone rogue, it must appear.
Lord, Lord, they resemble you not,
And I've got nothing left to fear.

ALMOST EVERY NIGHT

I woke up briefly
Sometime around 4 a.m.
After tossing and turning,
Roiling in turmoil
From images that I couldn't escape.
God, can I please rest?
Lord, please, just this once?
God, can I have one good dream?
I'd love to meet restful sleep.
Why must I always see the worst,
When my eyes close tight?
Please just let me rest,
Just for one night.

REFLECTED GHOSTS
For Michael

I saw a ghost in the reflection of your son.
Your eyes glinted from within him.
I saw an image, and that haunted me.
It cuts to the bone that you're gone,
And I'm just so damn angry.
There is simply no justice in poems or songs.
I miss you like Hell and it all feels wrong.
I just don't even know,
More questions than answers to show.
I saw a ghost, and it shook me to the bone.
An illusion of something they'll never get to know.
Your daughter has your smile, she's such a beauty.
I guess she'll have to hear about you from me.
Screaming at the steering wheel,
Waiting for any kind of confession.
But it doesn't grant me any concession.
A wedge split us as we grew.
God, I just don't get it, I forgot how much I loved you.
Now you're gone, leaving me here.
Tell me why, tell me why, why did you let it all go?
Tell me why, tell me why!
Why did you leave them both behind?
You may be dead but you live in both of their eyes,
Like reflected ghosts.

FUNERAL PRAYERS
For Whit

Hollow words,
And aimless affirmations
In the midst of grief.
Lying about prayers prayed.
Anger wells behind my eyes,
In saline streams of sadness.
God bring revival.
Bring back those sweet souls,
Lost to the depravity of church and state.
Is this endless cynicism
Our collective fate?
When you take the best and leave the filth
How can I even believe you're real?
I guess I still believe,
I'm just mad.
I wish you still cured.
I wish you still healed.
Are you even real?
Dissonance
Distance
Death
I'm sick of this race.
If you're with me,
To the end of the day,
To the end of an era,
Then why am I so alone,
So confused?
Lord, Lord, where are you?
Have I fallen away?

NARRATIVES

They've all got narratives.

Spinning politics,

Religion,

Science,

And all other gossip.

Each one

Articulating

Talking points

With no compassion.

Empathetic voids,

Overlapping speech,

Everyone's paranoid.

There are too many narratives,

And we all have a voice.

Man, these rabbit holes go deep.

SWORDS OF MY YOUTH

The swords of my youth

Now beaten into a plowshare

That cultivates my doubt.

Wrestling with God,

And the dissonance of war.

I look in the mirror,

And don't know that kid anymore.

ACT IV

ADULT PHASE

THERE'S NO BLOOD ON MY HANDS

There's no blood on my hands,

But I've killed you a thousand times.

My heart is weak from beating,

And my soul is tired from breathing.

Maybe I should just plan my own funeral

Because I've killed myself a thousand times

In this mind of mine.

I just sometimes wish,

Maybe, I'd never have been born,

Or never come home from the war.

Nothing is the same.

Nothing has been the same.

My better days are all yesterdays,

And today I lament my own existence.

Why does this darkness take hold?

Why can't I just soldier on?

Suck it up and drive on.

I've killed you a thousand times,

But there's no blood on my hands.

THAT BITCH, DEATH

First Published in *In Love...& War the Anthology of Poet Warriors Volume 1*

Death is a person.

She lingers and languishes around begging for attention.

She speaks with tracer rounds on the 1's and the 5's.

She daily clings close and I can't seem to shake her.

Left, right, left, right, left, right, her influences march through my brain.

She lures men to join her, never to again be among the living.

Shades wandering about, guided by Virgil in those rings of Hell.

She flows like a severed femoral artery,

And in less than 3 minutes she drains the life force out of once vibrant men.

Her stains pattern the sand, bloody reminders of what once was.

The tormentor of sleep, the hijacker of my waking hours.

She lures men to their graves and takes great pleasure in a job well done.

THE CYCLE REPEATS
Previously Published in *In Love...& War: The Anthology of Poet Warriors VOL I*

I'm doing that thing again.

The vicious cycle of self-loathing and narcissistic ambition.

Stuck in this loop of anxiety and energy.

I look down at my bare wrist where the watch usually sits

and realize my time is fading and

It's well past time for sleep.

Where do the hours go?

Where did the meaning all go?

My life used to have purpose but now just routine.

Wake up

Curse my insomnia

Blaspheme the little sleep I managed to bargain from the tormentors in my dreams.

Shower.

Dress.

Coffee.

Work.

Misanthropic nihilism.

Dinner.

Dwell.

Nightmare.

Repeat.

This cyclical journey of purposeless wealth acquisition

Only to divvy out my earnings to pay for things I don't have the time to enjoy.
The adventures of my youth now turn to a peppering of gray in my hair and beard.
Growing older and losing perspective of the dreams I once chased with reckless abandon.
Where did all that faith go?
How has my hope died?
Why did the man behind the curtain at Oz have to be a fraud?
Can someone please pull the wool over my sheepish sleep deprived sunken eyes?
I would rather be blissfully unaware than educated in the deceptions of church and state.
It's time for sleep.
Those nocturnal demons of wide-eyed stimuli
Perpetuating this vigilant awareness of my finite existence.
Close my eyes.
Bid my time.
Maybe tomorrow will be that elusive "One Day" that everything changes.

IN THE MIRROR

The enemy,

My main adversary,

Has been staring

Right at me.

Every time

I pass by the mirror,

He stares,

Right at me.

Longingly.

DISSONANCE

First Published in *In Love…& War the Anthology of Poet Warriors Volume 1*

When the dissonance turns to distance and I just can't handle this

When you're supposed to have it all figured out but you can't even get your own shit together

Breathe in

Breathe out

Sigh

No relief

No hope

No end

Swallow it down swallow it down

Bury the pain and pretend it's ok

Bury it down

No hope here

Just bury it down

You're a man

Be a man

Bury it down

Further

Deeper

Dead

DOOM SCROLLING

    Scroll

    Scroll

    Scroll

    Scroll

Always looking

Never Finding

    Scroll

    Scroll

    Scroll

    Scroll

SHOTGUN EPITAPH

Maybe I'll go out like Hemingway or Cobain,

By painting this wall with pieces of my brain.

Maybe I'll die, old and gray,

But I'm betting that'd be the day.

My cadence is out of sorts, and the rhythm is off-time.

Why does my mind always entertain such grime?

I suppose dying can be better than an existence austere.

Wishing my brain wasn't mostly to blame.

Maybe I'll go out like Hemingway or Cobain.

I REALLY DON'T WANT TO DIE

I really don't want to die.

It's just sometimes it's hard to breathe.

My heart races and I'm not me.

My head spins and darkness enters.

I really don't want to die.

I just want to feel good again.

I wish I could snap,

And cure this malady.

I wish I could just pray,

And it would all go away.

Life seems worth living,

When my head doesn't get in the way.

Despite the storm in my mind,

I really don't want to die.

THE WORLD IS ENDING

The world is ending,

That's what they say.

Polar ice caps,

Starting to melt away.

The world is ending,

That's what they yell.

Sinners dying,

Burning in Hell.

The world is ending,

I guess I should care.

Earth is dying,

Drowning polar bears.

The world is ending,

I'll just close my eyes.

What can I even do,

Besides hypothesize?

LOVE LETTERS TO DEATH

First Published in *In Love...& War the Anthology of Poet Warriors Volume 1*

I've been writing love letters to death.
I've been sending signals to the dead.
Wishing I could erase the dysfunction from my brain.
Hoping I can escape the darkness I've created.
I've been writing love letters to death,
But she doesn't seem to want to reply.
I beckon for her to come close,
But she stays just out of reach.
Siren songs of half-dead impulse lure my heart to despair.
I've been writing letters to death,
On wings of fallen angels.
Waiting to see them fly once again.
Broken wings defy aerodynamics, creating lift.
Out of the darkness,
Out of the depths,
I've been writing love letters to death.
But they all keep getting marked return to sender.
I'll keep my distance and walk to the light.
I'll close my eyes and pray for sleep this night.
I've been writing love letters to death,
But she doesn't seem to hear me.
I'll close my eyes tight,
And pray she's nowhere near me.
I've been writing love letters to death,
But she's not listening.
I'm done writing,
I'm ready to live.

MY BROTHER'S KEEPER

I'll carry you
Much longer than
The weight you can pull.
But when you stop trying,
And halt all progress,
The chore is much more
Than I'm willing to endure.
I'll help 'til the sun sets and goes black.
I'll drag you as you lay limp,
Carried slung across my back.
I won't let you give up,
And even when you do,
I'll pull you further still.
But there comes a time
When your encumbrance
Has to be shed like snake skin.
Because carrying you
Leaves us both dead in the end.
I can't dream for you and me too.
When making excuses is all you can do,
There comes a moment
When I must relent.
I'm spent and given all I can.
I'll have to walk the last mile alone.
I took you as far as I could.

COMPLAINTS

I'd rather

Hear your complaints

Than speak

At your funeral.

So, unburden yourself,

Pick up the phone,

Tell me your heartaches.

Reach out,

I'm always here.

Just reach out,

I'm dialing now.

It's too much,

To bear alone.

THE STRONG ONE

Who do you call

When you're falling apart?

When you're the one they call,

When they're torn in two.

Don't want to be a burden,

But a dial tone may be less

Burdensome than a mess

To clean up,

Long after I'm gone.

So maybe I'll dial,

And pray someone answers.

Needing only an ear,

Just to hear me vent.

So that they can share this weight

With me for a change,

And I can go on being

The "strong" one.

LOVE IN 4 LINES
For Jess

Endorphins rush.

Bride and groom both blush.

Years become a compounding blur.

But in the end, it was always her.

TODAY IS NOT THE DAY

Today is not the day

That my dreams come true.

But today is a day

I got to spend with you.

And sometimes, that's enough.

GREAT START

Great at starting,

Great at dreaming,

Great at hoping,

Great at planning,

But when it comes to finishing,

Great at procrastinating.

WEIRD DREAMS

Weird dreams

I can't seem

To remember

About real events

I can't seem

To forget.

I'VE GOT TWO FEET IN THE GRAVE

I've got two feet in the grave,

Trading blows with that old tormentor.

Yea, I've got two feet in the grave.

All I've got to do is smile,

But I'm no pretender

'Cause if I just quit,

Lay down and die,

Maybe my tombstone would stand

The test of trouble and time.

I've got two feet in the grave,

'Cause I've already died a myriad of times.

Inhale, exhale, accept my demons,

My defeat,

'Cause I'm standing on my own two feet,

But both are in the grave.

Life and death,

Just wrestling over my fate.

Both feet in the grave,

But today is not the day.

MONSTER

You have the power

To conquer

Any monster.

Even the ones

You make up.

LOSING SIGHT

I've lost sight
Of all the little things
That made me tick.
The little quirks
That once made me unique,
Now seem
To set my teeth on edge.
I've lost sight
Of my dreams,
I no longer dream.
I just replicate the day prior,
And put one foot in front of the other.
I wish I still had vision,
But sadly, I must admit,
I've lost sight.

GNATS ON THE WIND

On a dilapidated dock, I stood.
Feeling nervous about soggy splintered wood.
My mind roiled and raced, pondering its strength.
Across the marsh, it spanned a dizzying length.
I saw gnats dance as they swarmed.
It's hard to describe how my heart warmed.
It felt like nature, or maybe even God was speaking.
They seemed to know exactly what I was seeking.
I was enraptured by the beauty,
And more so by the simplicity.
Just some bugs gathered on the breeze.
Summer winds gently stir nearby trees.
That moment nearly brought me to tears.
Having struggled for a number of years,
The world seemed to go gray.
But, today, her full splendor was on display.
I saw beauty that was awe-inspiring.
I spent more than a moment just admiring.
I was humbled by the scope.
Such tiny animals, living unbeknown.
Happily performing their daily activities.
Hovering over sunset-painted lilies.
It was hard for me to focus with any clarity,
On the broken parts inside of me.

As I was bewildered by this sudden beauty.
Tiny pests dancing on the wind, as if they knew me.

SOMETIMES

Sometimes it sneaks up on me.

Moments of weakness,

Mental anguish.

Sometimes,

I even forget,

That I carry this weight.

Until unseen,

It makes me aware,

And then I remember.

It was always there.

Just under the surface,

Seething,

Teeming,

Growing wings,

Biting teeth.

Sometimes,

It sneaks up on me.

These doubts,

Insecurities,

Restlessness,

Anxiety.

I wish I was better.

Dear God,

I truly do wish.

So far,

I've always won,

Against these sneak attacks.

But I fear the day,

My guard will be down,

And you'll read about me

In the paper

Or some social media post.

I guess at least you're reading

That's all I ever wanted.

WHAT WEIGHT DOES A TREE CARRY?

Previously Published in *Understory: A Digital Zine for Relief in Western North Carolina (Loblolly Press)*

A Live Oak roils from the southern soil.
Festooned with wisteria blooms,
And a regal spreading crown.
Limbs reaching up,
And crawling back down.
A mass of long-suffering timber.
Generation after generation, she remembers,
Everything.

Sunlight shines on cicada's eyes.
June bugs are dazzling,
Sparkling by design.
Her glossy leaves are like summer jewels,
And the Spanish moss
Swaying softly on the breeze
Now keeps the time,
Rhythmically.

Oh, if they could tell us stories.
Oh, if this oak could talk.
I'd imagine we'd hear
Songs of the South.
Perhaps of triumph and tragedies alike.
The resurrection ferns cling,
On the bark's deep-cut glory,
Symbiotically.

As children, we swung on rope swings
From the same weighty boughs
On which men have also hung.
They swayed like a metronome,
One we'd rather not dance to.
A time we wish we could forget.
The oak remembers,
Tragically.

The live oak stands
Forcing confrontations of history.
Neither proud nor ashamed of the shade.
Below her mighty branches darkly splayed,
She provides comfort for Confederate dead.
There's also solace for field hands and their kin.
Her face shields the sun despite our many sins,
Thankfully.

What weight does a tree carry,
When men execute abysmal acts?
Kindness or hatred,
The tree stands all the same.
Oh, that must be a terrible burden.
Whether innocent or complicit,
The oak stood watch,
Faithfully.

BOTTLED UP

Previously Published in *Lethal Minds Journal*

Some stories stay

On the tip of my tongue,

As if nestled there

Never spoken or sung.

Things no one

Wants to hear.

Retelling trauma from

Bygone years.

Penned up, boarded,

Some stories stay

Closed off permanently.

It has to be this way.

I wish I could share,

Or even divulge,

But I'll swallow it down.

That terrible, tearful bulge.

War stories,

And youthful folly

Stay tied up

On tongues with faux jolly.

Bottled up,

And forced to the bottom

Because no one wants

To hear your problems.

EPILOGUE

Sometimes it feels like I have lived many separate lives. Growing up in the American Southeast, I engaged with the wonders of the world as a naturalist and sought wonder wherever I could find it. Our rich biodiversity has inspired a reverence and richness that often finds its way into my camera lens, notebooks–and sometimes my terrariums.

I have lived as an antagonistic atheist, arguing the merits of religion. Then, later, as a traveling preacher with a fiery faith, all while wrestling with deeply seated skepticism and doubt I couldn't shake. I've lived as a soldier called to serve during a time of war. With all the baggage that comes in the aftermath of such an experience, I've learned to distill those emotions on the page. The diverging of so many paths has created a cognitive dissonance and a longing for understanding. The poems in this collection made me evaluate what it means to be home, both physically in a place and metaphorically as a concept.

I've used the lessons learned in nature as a way to process the beauty of the world that is often juxtaposed with the ugliness that lives inside of us. In many poems, I use death as a device, a living entity at times, to explore the creative depths of depression and trauma. These poems are an attempt to drown out the static and process the competing storylines that jostle for prominence in my brain.

The theme of dissonance is a steady thread weaving its way throughout this collection. I have wrestled with the conflict of my wartime service, being both proud of my service and in disagreement with war as a whole. The contrast between my complete suspicion of the supernatural and my feeble attempts at faith wracks me with both curiosity and frustration. I dive into my fascination with death and the crippling depression that leads me to contemplate my own ending more than I'd like to admit. I even wrestle with the discord of loving nature and being helpless to save the environment I see decaying around me. There are no easy answers for me in this volume, and you will likely find it dizzying at times and hopefully comforting at others. I suspect there's little middle ground. Mostly, I hope that you find at least some of that mixture relatable. This collection is a visceral depiction of the chaos in my brain.

I have used poetry as a way to process emotions since I was a kid. I filled countless spiral-bound notebooks with the musings of adolescent angst, protest, and heartbreak. In 2009, I decided to start fresh. I burned my war journals, poetry notebooks, and old photo albums. I torched my entire creative past as a burnt offering on the altar of creativity in hopes of creating my best work moving forward.

If you've read my previous works regarding faith or my writings on nature, you may be in for a rude awakening. You may find yourself wondering how I can confidently write about theology in one collection and dive into despair in the next. Please understand that these poems offer you a view into the deepest parts of me. The parts that I've often been either too scared or too ashamed to acknowledge. I want you to recognize that although I do still claim to be a person of faith, I cannot in good conscience proclaim that I have it all figured out. These poems are profane, perverse, and often the darkest, most honest parts of me. By putting pen to paper, I bleed on the page, and it satisfies that doubt or hopelessness, and, in the moment, I can find clarity through introspection.

    I hope this collection not only resonates with you but also helps to open up a conversation about the myriad ways to overcome trauma. I hope it can show you that you're not alone if you can relate to the emotions held within these pages. Whether it be combat, or childhood, or anything in between, I hope that these words offer some salve for our collective wounds.

PREVIOUSLY PUBLISHED WORKS BY DEAD RECKONING COLLECTIVE:

FACT & MEMORY by: Tyler Carroll & Keith Dow

IN LOVE… &WAR: THE POET WARRIOR ANTHOLOGY VOL. 1

WAR… &AFTER: THE POET WARRIOR ANTHOLOGY VOL. 2

WAR{N}PIECES by: Leo Jenkins

LUCKY JOE by: Brian Kimber, Leo Jenkins, and David Rose

SOBER MAN'S THOUGHTS by: William Bolyard

KARMIC PURGATORY by: Keith Dow

WAR IS A RACKET by: Smedley Butler

THE FIRST MARAUDER by: Luke Ryan

WHERE THEY MEET by: Cokie

POPPIES by: Amy Sexauer

ROCK EATER by: Mason Rodrigue

REVISION OF A MAN by: Matt Smythe

ON ASSIMILATION by: Leo Jenkins

SANGIN, THEN AND NOW by Neville Johnson

A WORD LIKE GOD by Leo Jenkins

PHANTOMS by Ben Fortier

KILLERS IN THEIR YOUTH by Nicholas Efstathiou

DOUBLE KNOT by Mac Caltrider

DEMONS IN THE TAILLIGHTS by William Bolyard

ODYSSEUS AND THE OAR by Adam Magers

SCREAMING EAGLES WINGS by David Rose

THE TRANSCRIPT by Nick Orton

SOMETIMES I GO AWAY by Steven M Callahan

SO LONG: THE POET WARRIOR ANTHOLOGY VOL. 3

DEAD RECKONING COLLECTIVE is a veteran owned and operated publishing company. Our mission encourages literacy as a component of a positive lifestyle. Although DRC only publishes the written work of military veterans, the intention of closing the divide between civilians and veterans is held in the highest regard. By sharing these stories it is our hope that we can help to clarify how veterans should be viewed by the public and how veterans should view themselves.

>Visit us at:
>deadreckoningco.com

@deadreckoningcollective

@deadreckoningco

@DRCpublishing

PREVIOUSLY PUBLISHED WORKS BY STAN LAKE

The Not So Ordinary Journey of Todd the Toad

The Wonder of it All

The Halloween Traveler

Whispers in the Woods: An Invitation to Experience the Wonder of God's Creation

Follow Stan Lake

 @catchingcreation

STAN LAKE is a writer, photographer, and filmmaker currently living in Bethania, North Carolina with his wife Jess and their house full of animals. He split his time growing up between chasing wildlife and screaming on stages in hardcore bands you've never heard of. His work has been published in *The Havok Journal, Reptiles Magazine, Understory, Dirtbag Magazine, Lethal Minds Journal, Backcountry Journal, Wildlife in North Carolina, SOFLETE, The Tarheel Guardsman*, and others. He has written three children's books and one Christian devotional book. He filmed and directed a documentary called *Hammer Down* about his 2005 deployment in support of Operation Iraqi Freedom with Alpha Battery 5-113th of the NC Army National Guard. He spends most of his free time wrangling toads. You can see his collected works and social media accounts at *www.stanlakecreates.com*

www.ingramcontent.com/pod-product-compliance
Lightning Source LLC
Chambersburg PA
CBHW031632160426
43196CB00006B/386